MARIE CURIE

FERNANDO GORDON

Consulting Editor, Diane Craig, M.A./Reading Specialist

Super Sandcastle

An Imprint of Abdo Publishing
abdopublishing.com

abdopublishing.com

Published by Abdo Publishing, a division of ABDO, PO Box 398166, Minneapolis, Minnesota 55439. Copyright © 2017 by Abdo Consulting Group, Inc. International copyrights reserved in all countries. No part of this book may be reproduced in any form without written permission from the publisher. Super SandCastle™ is a trademark and logo of Abdo Publishing.

Printed in the United States of America, North Mankato, Minnesota
062016
092016

THIS BOOK CONTAINS RECYCLED MATERIALS

Editor: Rebecca Felix
Content Developer: Nancy Tuminelly
Cover and Interior Design and Production: Mighty Media, Inc.
Photo Credits: Bain News Service/Library of Congress; Getty Images; Library of Congress; Shutterstock; Wellcome Library, London; Wikimedia Commons

Library of Congress Cataloging-in-Publication Data
Names: Gordon, Fernando, author.
Title: Marie Curie / by Fernando Gordon ; consulting editor, Diane Craig,
  M.A./reading specialist.
Description: Minneapolis, Minnesota : Abdo Publishing, [2017] | Series:
  Scientists at work
Identifiers: LCCN 2016001415 (print) | LCCN 2016009202 (ebook) | ISBN
  9781680781540 (print) | ISBN 9781680775976 (ebook)
Subjects: LCSH: Curie, Marie, 1867-1934--Juvenile literature. | Women chemists
  --Poland--Biography--Juvenile literature. | Women chemists--France--Biography
  --Juvenile literature. | Nobel Prize winners--Biography--Juvenile literature. |
  Radioactivity--History--Juvenile literature.
Classification: LCC QD22.C8 G65 2017 (print) | LCC QD22.C8 (ebook) | DDC
  540.92--dc23
LC record available at http://lccn.loc.gov/2016001415

Super SandCastle™ books are created by a team of professional educators, reading specialists, and content developers around five essential components—phonemic awareness, phonics, vocabulary, text comprehension, and fluency—to assist young readers as they develop reading skills and strategies and increase their general knowledge. All books are written, reviewed, and leveled for guided reading, early reading intervention, and Accelerated Reader™ programs for use in shared, guided, and independent reading and writing activities to support a balanced approach to literacy instruction.

CONTENTS

GROUNDBREAKING SCIENTIST

Marie Curie was a famous scientist. She studied **chemistry** and **physics**. She found two new elements!

Marie Curie

MARIE CURIE

BORN: November 7, 1867, Warsaw, Poland

MARRIED: Pierre Curie, July 25, 1895

CHILDREN: Iréne Curie, Éve Curie

DIED: June 4, 1934, Sallanches, France

M. Curie

GROWING UP

Marie was born Maria Salomea Skłodowska. She grew up in Warsaw, Poland. Her father was a teacher. He taught Marie science.

The building in which Marie was born is now a museum.

A statue of Marie Curie in Warsaw

WORKING HARD

In 1885, Marie became a **governess.** She first worked in Warsaw. The next year, she took a governess job in a nearby village. Marie sent money to her older sister. The money helped her sister pay for college. Marie read science books in her spare time.

Marie (left) *and her sister Bronisława* (right)

MARIE THE STUDENT

In 1891, Marie went to college. Her sister helped pay for it. Marie moved to Paris, France. She began studying at the Sorbonne. Marie earned a **physics** degree in 1893. She earned a math degree the next year.

Marie worked in Gabriel Lippmann's laboratory at the Sorbonne. He was a famous physicist.

The Sorbonne in Paris

ARMANDVS · IOANNES · CARD · DVX · RICHELIVS · SORBONAE · PROVISOR
AEDIFICAVIT · DOMVM · ET · EXALTAVIT · TEMPLVM · S · DOMINO · MDCXLII

MEETING PIERRE

Marie met Pierre Curie in 1894. Pierre was a scientist like Marie. He was famous for his work in **physics**. Pierre and Marie soon got married. The Curies' work would change science forever.

Marie and Pierre Curie

Curie with her and Pierre's daughters, Éve (left) and Iréne (right)

A TERRIFIC TEAM

The Curies did experiments together. They also looked at work from other scientists. Henri Becquerel was a **physicist**. He studied **uranium** in 1897. He saw that it gave off energy.

Uranium ore

Henri Becquerel

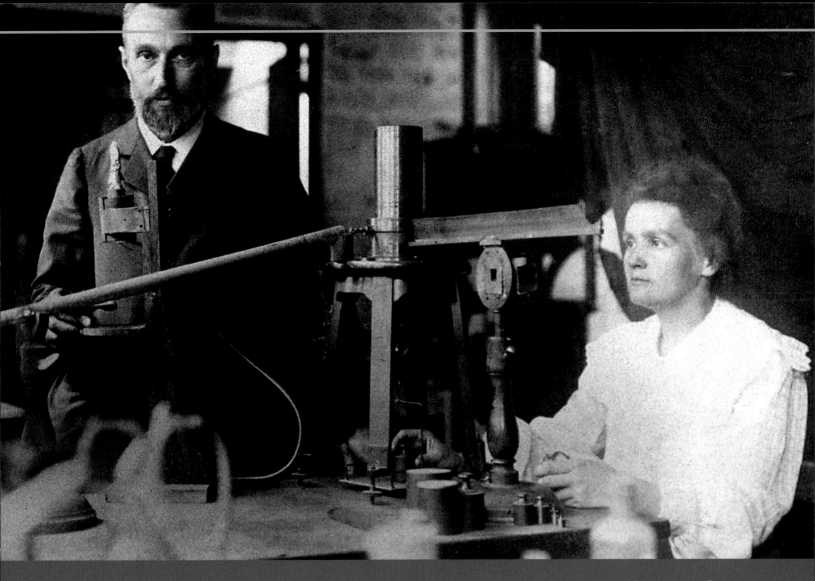

The Curies wanted to know more. Did other elements give off energy?

The couple wanted to find out. The Curies started their own experiments.

A GREAT DISCOVERY

In 1898 Curie found two new elements. She named one polonium. The other was radium. Both gave off energy. Curie called this energy **radiation**.

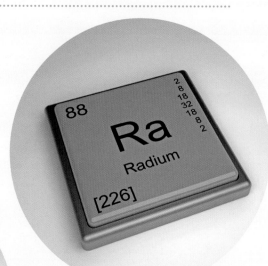

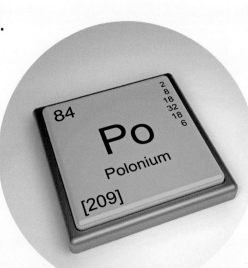

Curie won a **Nobel Prize** in **physics** in 1903. She shared it with Becquerel and Pierre.

Pierre and Curie

TEACHING SCIENCE

The Curies were now famous. Pierre began teaching at the Sorbonne. They continued their experiments. Then **tragedy** struck. Pierre died in 1906.

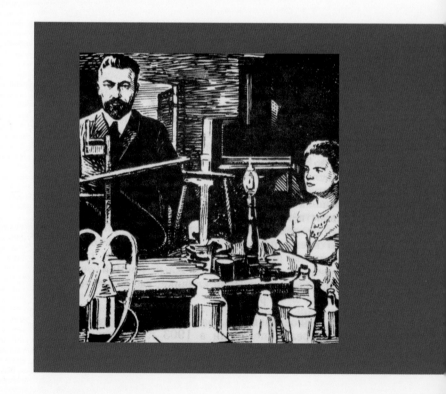

Curie took over his classes. And she kept experimenting on her own.

Curie was the first woman to teach at the Sorbonne.

A LIFETIME OF DISCOVERY

Curie won a second **Nobel Prize** in 1911. This prize was in **chemistry**. Curie never stopped working. She invented a **mobile X-ray** machine. It was used during World War I (1914–1918).

Curie's daughter Iréne helped her with her work.

Curie died in 1934.
But her discoveries
changed science
forever.

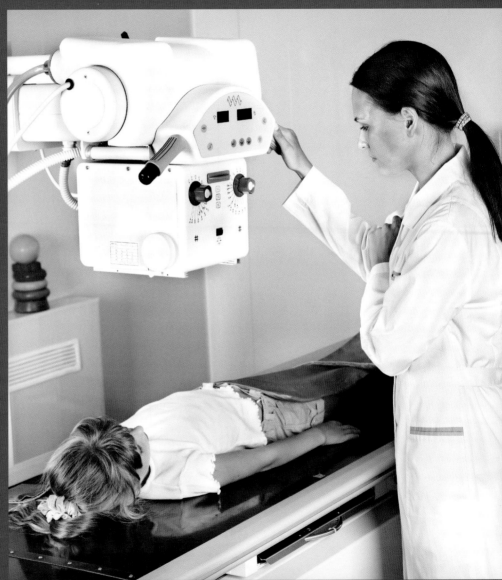

*Curie's work led to
the X-ray machines
we use today!*

MORE ABOUT CURIE

Curie was the FIRST WOMAN to win a **Nobel Prize**.

Curie's DAUGHTER IRÉNE also won a Nobel Prize.

At night, the Curies' laboratory GLOWED BLUE from the **radiation** of their samples.

TEST YOUR KNOWLEDGE

1. At what university did Marie Curie study, and later teach?

2. Curie discovered **uranium**.
True or false.

3. How many **Nobel Prizes** did Curie win?

THINK ABOUT IT!

Have you ever had an **X-ray** taken? What was it like?

ANSWERS: 1. The Sorbonne 2. False 3. Two

GLOSSARY

chemistry – the study of substances and what they are made of.

governess – a woman whose job is to teach children in their home.

mobile – able to be easily moved.

Nobel Prize – any of six yearly awards given for outstanding achievement in arts and sciences.

physics – the science of how energy and objects affect each other. Someone who studies physics is a physicist.

radiation – dangerous and powerful energy particles that are given off by something.

tragedy – a very sad and surprising event.

uranium – a chemical element that gives off radiation and can be used to produce nuclear energy.

X-ray – a photograph of the inside of the body or another object.